The Leader's Little Quote Book

COMPILED BY
Eric Ferguson

The Leader's Little Quote Book

Compiled by Eric Ferguson

Metanoia Missions International

ISBN 978-0-9838105-2-0

Printed in the United States of America

© Metanoia Missions International 2012

All rights reserved. No portion of this book may be reproduced in any form without the written permission of the author.

Cover photo by © Lorinda Gray

Book design by Lorinda Gray/Ragamuffin Creative
www.ragamuffincreative.com

Instruct the wise,
and they will be even wiser.
Teach the righteous and
they will learn even more.
—KING SOLOMON

What is important is ideas.
If you have ideas, you have the
main asset you need, and there isn't
any limit to what you can do with
your business and your life.
—HARVEY FIRESTONE

The best way to predict
the future is to create it.

—PETER DRUCKER

People with honor
don't need an honor code.
People without honor
won't heed an honor code.

—JEFFREY J. FOX

The sure way to miss success
is to miss the opportunity.

—VICTOR CHASLES

The difference between ordinary
and extraordinary is that little extra.
—ZIG ZIGLAR

If you lead people with correctness,
who will dare not to be correct?
—CONFUCIUS

Vision.
Get one.
Go with it.
Or get out of the way!
—E. FERGUSON

The reason most major goals are not achieved is that we spend our time doing second things first.

—ROBERT J. MCKAIN

Try not to become men of success.
Rather, become men of value.

—ALBERT EINSTEIN

All things are possible until they are proved impossible
—and even the impossible may only be so, as of now.

—PEARL S. BUCK

The right man is the one
who seizes the moment.

—GOETHE

Every time a person puts an idea across,
he finds ten people who thought about it
before he did—but they only thought about it.

—ALFRED MONTAPERT

Attitudes are more important than facts.

—KARL MENNINGER, M.D.

We are not only called to be changed and to
embrace change but to be the catalysts of change.
—ERWIN RAPHAEL M^CMANUS

I will pay more for the ability to handle people
than for any other talent under the sun.
—JOHN D. ROCKEFELLER

If you have the will to win,
you have achieved half your success;
if you don't, you have achieved half your failure.
—DAVID AMBROSE

A person of integrity is one who has established
a system of values against which all of life is judged.
—V. GILBERT BEERS

We live. We die. The best we can do is leave
a worthwhile example for those who come after us.
—ADAM WALINSKY

Always give without remembering
and always receive without forgetting.
—BRIAN TRACY

It takes more courage to reveal insecurities
than to hide them, more strength to relate to
people than to dominate them, more "manhood" to
abide by thought-out principles rather than blind reflex.
—ALEX KARRAS

Inventories can be managed,
but people must be led.
—H. ROSS PEROT

Leaders are visionaries with a poorly developed sense
of fear and no concept of the odds against them.
They make the impossible happen.
—DR. ROBERT JARVIK

We all live under the same sky,
but we don't all have the same horizon.
—KONRAD ADENAUER

Life is not so much a matter
of position as of disposition.
—UNKNOWN

When you believe in something,
and you carry it in your heart,
accept no excuses, only results.
—KEN BLANCHARD

It's hard to lead a cavalry charge
if you think you look funny on a horse.
—ALDAI STEVENSON

The gem cannot be polished without friction,
nor can man perfected without trials.
—CHINESE PROVERB

Example is the school of mankind,
and they will learn at no other.
—EDMUND BURKE

Don't let yesterday take up
too much of today.
—WILL ROGERS

In order to do more,
I've got to be more.
—JIM ROHN

The ability to keep a cool head in an emergency,
maintain poise in the midst of excitement, and to
refuse to be stampeded are true marks of leadership.
—R. SHANNON

The first great gift we can bestow
on others is a good example.
—THOMAS MORELL

You seldom get what you go after
unless you know in advance what you want.
—MAURICE WITZER

If your vision is for a year, plant wheat.
If your vision is for ten years, plant trees.
If your vision is for a lifetime, plant people.
—CHINESE PROVERB

Leadership can be thought of as a capacity
to define oneself to others in a way that clarifies
and expands a vision of the future.
—EDWIN H. FRIEDMAN

People don't care how much you know
until they know how much you care.
—DR. JOHN C. MAXWELL

Your spark can become a flame
and change everything.
—E.D. NIXON

Excellence demands that you be
better than yourself.
—TED ENGSTROM

The secret of success in this life is for a man
to be ready for his time when it comes.
—BENJAMIN DISRAELI

The world of achievement has always
belonged to the optimists.
—J. HAROLD WILKINS

One who fears failure limits his activities.
Failure is only the opportunity more
intelligently to begin again.
—HENRY FORD

The first method for estimating the intelligence
of a ruler is to look at the men he has around him.
—NICCOLÒ MACHIAVELLI

You can't make the other fellow feel important
in your presence if you secretly feel that he is a nobody.
—LES GIBLIN

The only safe ship in
a storm is leadership.
—FAYE WATTLETON

No man can climb out beyond
the limitations of his own character.
—JOHN MORELY

It's much easier to be very busy
than to be very effective.
—A. ROGER MERRILL

There is something that is much more scarce,
something rarer than ability.
It is the ability to recognize ability.
—ROBERT HALF

Organization is something
you have to do everyday.
—FELICIA RAND

The person who knows "how" will always have a job.
The person who knows "why" will always be his boss.
—DIANE RAVITCH

A leader must have the courage
to act against an expert's advice.
—JAMES CALLAGHAN

Doing the right thing is more important
than doing things right.
—PETER DRUCKER

Do what you can,
with what you have,
where you are.
—TEDDY ROOSEVELT

The world belongs to risk-takers.
—UNKNOWN

Everyone has an invisible sign hanging
from his neck saying Make Me Feel Important!
Never forget this message when working with people.
—MARY KAY ASH

Leader-ship. A good leader leads the ship
from port into uncharted waters.
An unqualified leader simply leaves
the port and sinks the ship.
Where's your ship headed?
—E. FERGUSON

You don't motivate people,
you influence what they're motivated to do.
—JOHN WOODS

Management is efficiency in climbing
the ladder of success; leadership determines
whether the ladder is leaning against the right wall.
—STEPHEN R. COVEY

Every job is a self-portrait
of the person who does it.
Autograph your work with excellence.
—UNKNOWN

The best organizations
create a culture of leaders.
—F. HESSELBEIN

True leaders are able to influence
not only individuals, but also environments.
—ERWIN RAPHAEL MCMANUS

The measure of man is not in the number
of his servants, but in the number
of people whom he serves.
—PAUL D. MOODY

The very essence of leadership is
that you have to have a vision.
—THEODORE HESBURGH

Do all the good you can, in all the ways you can,
to all the souls you can, in every place you can,
at all the times you can, with all the zeal you can,
as long as ever you can.
—JOHN WESLEY

Sight sees that which is visible and present,
vision sees that which is invisible and yet to be.
—MICHAEL HODGIN

Optimism is the faith
that leads to achievement.
—HELEN KELLER

Leaders must encourage their organizations
to dance to forms of music yet to be heard.
—WARREN G. BENNIS

Example is always more
efficacious than precept.
—SAMUEL JOHNSON

It is amazing how much people can get done
if they do not worry about who gets the credit.
—SANDRA SWINNEY

Change is an excellent catalyst for growth,
for both you and your organization,
so do not fear it, embrace it.
—E. FERGUSON

Be the change you want to see in the world.
—MAHATMA GANDHI

Attitudes are nothing more than
habits of thought, and habits can be acquired.
An action repeated becomes an attitude realized.
—PAUL MEIER

The true meaning of a person is not to be
found in the person himself, but in the
changes that happen in others because of him.
—A.L. SCHWIEKGER

If you put off everything till you're sure of it,
you'll get nothing done.
—NORMAN VINCENT PEALE

The quality of a leader is reflected
in the standards they set for themselves.
—RAY KROC

There is no more noble occupation in the world
than to assist another human being—
to help someone succeed.
—ALAN McGINNIS

Take calculated risks.
That is quite different from being rash.
—GEORGE S. PATTON

People don't resist change as much
as the implications of change.
—D.R. CONNOR

You will be tomorrow
what you are planning for today.
—UNKNOWN

The best helping hand you will ever find
is at the end of your own arm.
—JOHN MASON

The art of leadership is saying no, not yes.
It is very easy to say yes.
—TONY BLAIR

Nothing is politically right
which is morally wrong.
—DANIEL O'CONNELL

He who has a why to live for
can bear almost any how.
—FREDRICK NEITZCHE

The way to be nothing
is to do nothing.
—EDGAR W. HOWE

The glory of great men must always be measured
against the means they have used to acquire it.
—FRANCOIS DUC DE LA ROCHEFOUCAULD

God has a tailor-made plan for you
and you are being tailored to fit His plan.
—UNKNOWN

Remember the difference
between a boss and a leader:
a boss says "Go!"—
a leader says "Let's go!"
—E.M. KELLY

The rung of the ladder was never
meant to rest upon, but to enable
a man to put his other foot higher.
—THOMAS HUXLEY

Until you make peace with who you are,
you will never be content with what you have.
—DORIS MORTMAN

Our greatest limitation
is not the leader above us,
but the spirit within us.
—DR. JOHN C. MAXWELL

Indecision is often worse
than wrong action.
—GERALD FORD

Love produces servanthood.
Servanthood sees sacrifice as a privilege.
—ERWIN RAPHAEL McMANUS

God's alarm clock has no snooze button.
You postpone your life when
you can't make up your mind.
—UNKNOWN

Readers are leaders.
—WARREN BENNIS

Don't be afraid to fail.
Don't waste energy trying to cover up failure.
If you're not failing, you're not growing.
—H. STANLEY JUDD

We get the leaders we create.
—PETER BLOCK

Leaders need to spend less time in the present
and more time inhabiting the future.
—ELLEN R. HART

Experience is not what happens to a man.
It is what a man does with what happens to him.
—ALDOUS HUXLEY

Leadership is an active, living process.
It is rooted in character, forged by experience,
and communicated by example.

—JOHN BALDONI

Devoting a little of yourself to everything means
committing a great deal of yourself to nothing.

—MICHAEL LEBOEF

Hold yourself responsible for a higher
standard than anyone else expects of you.
Never excuse yourself.
Never pity yourself.
Be a hard master to yourself—
and lenient to everybody else.

—HENRY WARD BEECHER

To manage men, one ought to have
a sharp mind in a velvet sheath.
—GEORGE ELIOT

You have no right to complain
about what you permit.
—MIKE MURDOCK

People have a way of becoming
what you encourage them to be—
not what you nag them to be.
—SCUDDER N. PARKER

You can have a mission without a leader,
but no leader without a mission.
—SONJA MARTINS DIAS

An honest heart being the first blessing,
a knowing head is the second.
—THOMAS JEFFERSON

Happy are those who dream dreams
and are ready to pay the price
to make them come true.
—LEON J. SUENENS

It is the nature of man to rise to greatness
if greatness is expected of him.
—JOHN STEINBECK

Any man who selects a goal in life
which can be fully achieved has
already defined his own limitations.
—CAVETT ROBERT

A man of character finds special attractiveness
in difficulty, since it is only by coming to
grips with difficulty that he can
realize his potentialities.
—CHARLES DE GAULLE

People know what you care about
by what you are willing to die for.
—ERWIN RAPHAEL McMANUS

Faith dares the soul to go
farther than it can see.
—WILLIAM CLARK

Life's most persistent and urgent question is,
"What are we doing for others?"
—MARTIN LUTHER KING JR.

More men fail
through lack of purpose
than lack of talent.

—BILLY SUNDAY

You'd better know what you want,
because you'll probably get it.

—DAN GREENBURG

The mature person meets the demands
of life, while the immature person
expects life to meet their demands.

—HENRY CLOUD

Greatness lies not in being strong,
but in the right using of strength.
—HENRY WARD BEECHER

What lies behind us and
what lies before us are
tiny matters compared
to what lies within us.
—RALPH WALDO EMERSON

People who say it cannot be
done should not interrupt
those who are doing it.
—UNKNOWN

If I see people around me succeeding,
it will stimulate my desire to succeed.
—DAVID KOLB

Character is not made in crisis;
it is only exhibited.
—UNKNOWN

Some men see things as they are and say,
"Why?" I dream of things that
never were and say, "Why not?"
—GEORGE BERNARD SHAW

Vision is the art of seeing things invisible.
—JONATHAN SWIFT

The final test of a leader
is that he leaves behind in others
the conviction and will to carry on.
—WALTER LIPPMAN

To be what we are, and to become
what we are capable of becoming,
is the only end of life.
—ROBERT LOUIS STEVENSON

The price of greatness is responsibility.
—WINSTON CHURCHILL

When your memories are greater
than your dreams, you are
already beginning to die.
—UNKNOWN

Don't fear failure so much that you
refuse to try new things. The saddest
summary of life contains three descriptions;
could have, might have, and should have.
—LOUIS BOONE

Striving for success without hard work
is like trying to harvest
where you haven't planted.

—DAVID BLY

To be upset over what you don't have
is to waste what you do have.

—KEN KEYS, JR.

Thoughts lead on to purposes;
purposes go forth in actions;
actions form habits;
habits decide character;
and character fixes our destiny.

—TRYON EDWARDS

Admitting errors clears the score
and proves you wiser than before.
—ARTHUR GUITERMAN

We set young leaders up for a fall
if we encourage then to envision
what they can do before they consider
the kind of person they shall be.
—R. RUTH BARTON

Who you are speaks so loudly
I can't hear what you're saying.
—RALPH WALDO EMERSON

Never let what your eyes see
determine what your heart believes.
—UNKNOWN

Your greatest challenge is not
in choosing between good and bad
but between good and the best.
—DR. MYLES MUNROE

No man can climb beyond the
limitations of his own belief.
—UNKNOWN

A dream can be wrecked by the
very passion and energy that fuel it,
if the dream is not managed correctly.
—TOMMY BARNETT

That which holds our attention
determines our actions.
—WILLIAM JAMES

You will become as small as your
controlling desire, as great as
your dominant aspiration.
—JAMES ALLEN

Nothing is so embarrassing
as watching someone do something
that you said could not be done.
—SAM EWING

Leadership is the capacity to
translate vision into reality.
—WARREN G. BENNIS

Never give an order
that can't be obeyed.
—GENERAL DOUGLAS MACARTHUR

Leadership is practiced not so much
in words as in attitude and action.
—HAROLD S. GREEN

A successful man is one who can
lay a firm foundation with the
bricks others have thrown at him.
—DAVID BRINKLEY

Change your thoughts
and you change your world.
—NORMAN VINCENT PEALE

It is easier to fight for one's principles
than to live up to them.
—ALFRED ADLER

Mountaintops inspire leaders
but valleys mature them.
—WINSTON CHURCHILL

Leaders make decisions that
create the future they desire.
—MIKE MURDOCK

The place to improve the world is first
in one's own heart and head and hands.
—ROBERT M. PIRSIG

The real leader has no need to lead—
he is content to point the way.
—HENRY MILLER

To become truly great,
one has to stand with people,
not above them.
—CHARLES DE MONTESQUIEU

Treat people as if they were
what they ought to be, and
you help them to become
what they are capable of being.
—JOHANN WOLFGANG VON GOETHE

A person, who no matter how
desperate the situation, gives
others hope, is a true leader.
—DAISAKU IKEDA

Personal leadership is not a singular experience.
It is, rather, the ongoing process of keeping your
vision and values before you and aligning your life
to be congruent with those most important things.
— STEPHEN COVEY

To be able to lead others, a man must
be willing to go forward alone.
— HARRY TRUMAN

Earn your success based on service to others,
not at the expense of others.
— H. JACKSON BROWN, JR

When a goal matters enough to a person
that person will find a way to accomplish
what at first seemed impossible.
—NIDO QUBEIN

Leaders need to be optimists.
Their vision is beyond the present.
—RUDY GIULIANI

To help others become something
that they could never on their own become,
is putting value into that other person.
—UNKNOWN

Don't be afraid to take a big step
when one is indicated.
You can't cross a chasm
in two small steps.
—DAVID LOYD GEORGE

The trouble is, if you don't risk
anything, you risk even more.
—ERICA JONG

Not everything that is faced can be changed.
But nothing can be changed until it is faced.
—JAMES BALDWIN

Do not follow where the path may lead.
Go instead where there is no path and leave a trail.
—HAROLD R. M^cALINDON

If your actions inspire others
to dream more, learn more,
do more and become more,
you are a leader.
—JOHN QUINCY ADAMS

Dream no small dreams
for they have no power
to move the hearts of men.
—GOETHE

The will to win is worthless
if you do not have the will to prepare.
—THANE YOST

Never . . . Never . . . Never . . . Never Give up!
—WINSTON CHURCHILL

As a leader you should always start with where people are before you try to take them to where you want them to go.
— JIM ROHN

A single lie destroys a whole reputation for integrity.
—BALTASAR GRACIAN

An army of deer would be more
formidable commanded by a lion,
than an army of lions commanded by a stag.

—VIKING PROVERB

A most important key to successful
leadership is your ability to direct
and challenge the very best that
is in those whom you lead.

—ANONYMOUS

Character is like a tree and
reputation like its shadow.
The shadow is what we think of it;
the tree is the real thing.

—ABRAHAM LINCOLN

The greatest discovery of my generation
is that a human being can alter his life
by altering his attitudes of mind.
—WILLIAM JAMES

Those who dream by day are cognizant
of many things which escape those
who dream only by night.
—EDGAR ALLAN POE

The final test of a leader is that
he leaves behind in other men the
conviction and the will to carry on.
—WALTER LIPPMAN

www.ingramcontent.com/pod-product-compliance
Lightning Source LLC
Chambersburg PA
CBHW070457050426
42449CB00012B/3021